CALORIES DON'T COUNT IF YOU EAT STANDING UP

and other diet tips

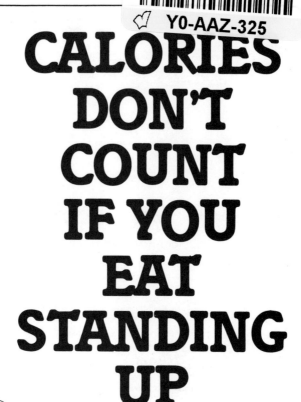

Written by
Barbara Gibbons

Designed and Illustrated by
Martin Riskin

Composition by
Wayne Geehan

CALORIES DON'T COUNT IF YOU EAT STANDING UP

Copyright © 1981 and 1982

By IVORY TOWER PUBLISHING COMPANY, INC.
(Former Copyright by American Publishing Corp.)

All Rights Reserved

Published simultaneously in Canada by
Encore Sales Inc. of Downsview, Ontario.

Manufactured in the United States of America.

IVORY TOWER PUBLISHING COMPANY, INC.
125 Walnut Street, Watertown, Massachusetts 02172
TEL: (617) 923-1111   TELEX: 955-439 Intel. Div. - ITOP

3

CALORIES DON'T COUNT IF YOU EAT STANDING UP

This relates to the
"Postural Dispensation" theory
of dieting which holds that
food (or drink) consumed
in a vertical position
bypasses the digestive system
and is changed into
electrical energy that flows
through the feet.
Note: for best results,
wear open-toed shoes.

CALORIES DON'T COUNT IN THE DARK

What you don't see
can't hurt you.
For caloric purposes,
semi-darkness will suffice.
Mallomars consumed in front
of the television set or
buttered popcorn at the movies
have no calories.
It is possible to enjoy an
entire seven course banquet,
if the candlelight is
sufficiently dim.

CALORIES DON'T COUNT AFTER MIDNIGHT

Provided you **don't** turn
on the kitchen light,
and **do** close the freezer door
after removing the ice cream.
(See "Calories Don't Count . . .
in the Dark.")

CALORIES DON'T COUNT IF IT DOESN'T TASTE GOOD

Only enjoyable food has calories; therefore, an overdone (or underdone) steak is calorie-free. So is strawberry ice cream, if they're out of butter pecan. The wrong brand of salad dressing negates the calories of the entire meal.

CALORIES DON'T COUNT IF YOU PUT IT IN PITA BREAD

"**P**ita" is the Middle Eastern word for "no calories." Pita bread forms a pocket in the intestines, trapping any calories consumed.

CALORIES DON'T COUNT IF THEY'RE NOT ON YOUR PLATE

Keep in mind the "Possession Rule" of weight maintenance: other people's food has no calories. If your dining companion orders cheesecake and you eat half of it, your partner will gain all the weight.

Donuts, potato chips or Mars Bars purchased in the name of minor children remain the caloric possession of those children, regardless who eats them.

CALORIES DON'T COUNT IF YOU ADD BEANSPROUTS

Beansprouts absorb the
energy (calories) from
any foods they are
combined with.

CALORIES DON'T COUNT IN CALIFORNIA

It is against California state law to serve food in any place of public accommodation without beansprouts.

CALORIES DON'T COUNT IF IT'S PART OF YOUR HERITAGE

"Ethnic" foods are calorie free, but only if you have a genetically-inherited resistance. Therefore, it is permissible to eat lasagna, if you're Italian but not if you're Polish. Unless you're married to an Italian. Anyone whose name ends in "ski" may consume Kielbasy. Note: caloric immunity is relinquished if you change or shorten your name. People named Green may not eat blintzes without suffering the caloric consequences.

CALORIES DON'T COUNT ON LEGAL HOLIDAYS

But this rule applies only to the appropriate foods. Corn on the cob is calorie-free on the Fourth of July, but cranberry sauce consumed on that day would be fattening. Nothing has calories between Thanksgiving and New Years.

CALORIES DON'T COUNT IF IT'S MADE WITH YOGURT

The live cultures in yogurt
consume the calories in any
combination of ingredients it's added to.
For this reason, it's wise to
consider adding a level tablespoon
of yogurt to cake mix.

CALORIES DON'T COUNT IF IT'S RELIGIOUS

Consider it an act of God:
the calories are miraculously
transformed in Hot Cross Buns,
Manischewitz wine, chocolate bunnies
and Christmas cookies.
(See also "Ethnic Foods")

CALORIES DON'T COUNT IF YOU EAT IN A HURRY

By their very nature, "fast foods" have no calories. (See "Calories Don't Count . . . If It Doesn't Taste Good.") Rushing through a meal minimizes the absorption of calories. If you have ordered dessert and now regret it, gobble it down.

CALORIES DON'T COUNT IF IT'S GOOD FOR YOU

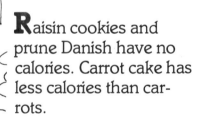

SALE
RAISIN
COOKIES

Raisin cookies and prune Danish have no calories. Carrot cake has less calories than carrots.

CALORIES DON'T COUNT IF IT'S FREE

Samples are calorie free.
This includes complimentary candies
left on your pillow by the
hotel maid, free mints at the
restaurant cash register,
sample slices at the cheese store.
Supermarket grapes have no
calories until they pass the check-out.

CALORIES DON'T COUNT ON THE AMERICAN PLAN

Always try to vacation at resorts
where meals are included
as part of the price
since you won't need to incur
any extra costs (or calories) for food.
Cruises are particularly beneficial.
Not only is the food generous
and (calorie) free, the salt air
helps dissolve fat deposits.

CALORIES DON'T COUNT IF YOU DRESS ATHLETICALLY

Anything eaten while wearing
tennis shorts, jogging pants
or a ski jacket is immediately
metabolized. Ice cream
eaten on the beach has no
calories if your swimsuit
is one piece.

CALORIES DON'T COUNT ON THE EXPENSE ACCOUNT

Business lunches are calorically deductible. Anything you eat (or drink) at an office party is non-fattening. It is poor employee relations to turn down a slice of your co-worker's birthday cake, cookies served at a going-away party.

CALORIES DON'T COUNT IF YOU EAT IN MOTION

Airline food has no calories to speak of. (See "Food That Doesn't Taste Good.") Anything eaten in the car has no calories whether the car is moving or not. Food eaten at drive-in movies creates a negative calorie balance. (See "Food Eaten in the Dark.")

CALORIES DON'T COUNT IF THEY'RE MEDICINAL

Mother's chicken soup has no calories during the flu season. Also included: sleep inducers like hot cocoa, tranquilizers like warm milk and brownies, pain-killers like Oreo cookies . . . brandy for cramps, Scotch to settle your nerves.

CALORIES DON'T COUNT IF SOMEBODY'S FEELINGS ARE AT STAKE

Anything somebody makes
"just for you" will not
make you fat.
This includes your mother's
chocolate chip cookies and
your favorite pie.
Your sensitivity to people's
feelings will be rewarded.

CALORIES DON'T COUNT IF THEY'RE GIFT WRAPPED

Chocolates in heart-shaped
boxes are always calorie free;
so is any booze with a
Christmas bow on it.
Anything anybody brings to
your house is calorically reduced
regardless of the wrapping,
and must be consumed in
their presence.
(See "Calories Don't Count . . .
If Somebody's Feelings
Are at Stake.")

CALORIES DON'T COUNT IF IT'S FOR CHARITY

Included in this group of
calorie-free foods are
Girl Scout cookies,
PTA bake sale cakes,
anything consumed at a fundraiser.
Foods eaten to save the
starving children are
always calorie free.

CALORIES DON'T COUNT IF YOU DRINK DIET SODA

A hot dog and French fries
washed down with Tab is
calorie free because the
saccharin in the soda dissolves
the fat in the food and
flushes it out of your system.
Light beer negates the calories in pretzels.
Ordering Perrier water not
only makes you slimmer,
it makes everybody else
look fat.

CALORIES DON'T COUNT IF THE SALAD BAR IS INCLUDED

It's a Board of Health regulation.

CALORIES DON'T COUNT IF IT'S THE LOCAL SPECIALTY

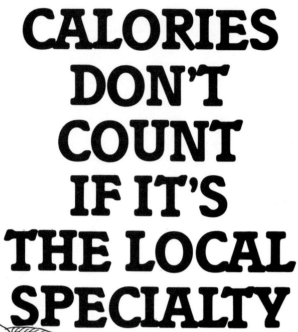

Baked beans are non-fattening in Boston; cream cheese is calorie free in Philadelphia; soft shelled crabs are non-caloric in Maryland. Chili is slimming in Texas. "Local" is an abbreviation for "low-calorie."

CALORIES DON'T COUNT IF YOU'RE TRYING TO QUIT SMOKING

The Surgeon General has determined that overeating is less harmful to your health.

CALORIES DON'T COUNT IF YOU KNOW THEM

Merely stating the calorie count out loud causes the calories to evaporate in the food you're about to eat. You can further enhance weight loss and cause a calorie deficit by pointing out the calorie counts of other people's food.

CALORIES DON'T COUNT IF YOU CHOOSE THE LESS FATTENING ALTERNATIVE

If you choose pumpkin pie (240 calories) instead of mincemeat (320 calories), the net calorie cost to you will be the difference between the item given up and the alternative (320 − 240 = 80). You can reduce the calories in a Peter Paul Mounds Bar to only four by choosing it instead of an Almond Joy.

CALORIES DON'T COUNT IF YOU'RE CLEANING THE REFRIGERATOR

The longer food is held at 40 degrees, the lower its calorie count. Read your owner's manual!

CALORIES DON'T COUNT IF YOU PUT IT IN THE BLENDER

The physical energy (calories) of food is released when the molecules are split. (Tech. ref.: Theory of Relativity — Einstein, Myron)

CALORIES DON'T COUNT DURING ATHLETIC ACTIVITIES

Physical activity burns up caloric energy: therefore, all hot dogs consumed in baseball stadiums are calorie-free. So are peanuts consumed watching the Superbowl. To eliminate the calories in pretzels, ask the bartender for odds on tomorrow's fight.

CALORIES DON'T COUNT AFTER SEX

(See Calories Don't Count During Athletic Activities.) There is no time limit to this dispensation.

CALORIES DON'T COUNT IF IT'S NOT IN YOUR CALORIE COUNTER

Macadamia nuts, Reese's Peanut Butter Cups and Enchiladas Con Queso, are among the foods you can safely assume to be calorie-free because they're not listed. For convenience and portability, it's best to select a compact calorie guidebook, small enough to fit in your wallet, preferably costing no more than 25¢.

CALORIES DON'T COUNT IF IT'S FROM YOUR GARDEN

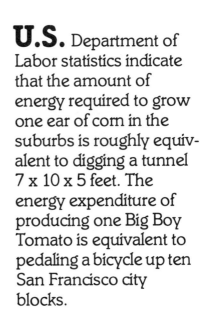

U.S. Department of Labor statistics indicate that the amount of energy required to grow one ear of corn in the suburbs is roughly equivalent to digging a tunnel 7 x 10 x 5 feet. The energy expenditure of producing one Big Boy Tomato is equivalent to pedaling a bicycle up ten San Francisco city blocks.

CALORIES DON'T COUNT IF YOU'RE FEEDING THE BABY

Food consumed for demonstration purposes is calorie-free, choo-choo train chocolate pudding for example. It is not necessary for the baby to be present. (See Calories Don't Count If You're Eating for Two.)

CALORIES DON'T COUNT IF YOU'RE EATING FOR TWO

And there's always the possibility of twins, or triplets.

CALORIES DON'T COUNT IF IT'S INTENDED FOR GARNISH

Icing roses, maraschino cherries and chocolate sprinkles are not food. They needn't be computed in your caloric bookkeeping.

CALORIES DON'T COUNT IF IT'S IN FRENCH

It's a popular misconception that French food is fattening; if you doubt this, look at the French models photographed in Vogue. The basic culinary technique of French cuisine is flambéeing, which eliminates calories by igniting them. The prices of entrees on French menus equate with the calories eliminated. To lose ten pounds in one week, consult Air France or see your travel agent.

CALORIES DON'T COUNT IF IT'S IMPORTED

International trade agreements require that the caloric value of foods remain the property of the exporting nation. That's why it's illegal to bring foreign foods home in your suitcase.

CALORIES DON'T COUNT IF IT'S EXPENSIVE

Overweight is rarely a problem with people in the upper rungs of the economic ladder because they dine on the most expensive selections (see Calories Don't Count If It's Imported). To feed your family for less (calories), shop in the supermarket on the other side of town.

OTHER NO- AND LOW- CALORIE FOODS

Anything labeled "natural" is calorie free. "Granola" is the Indian word for non-fattening.

Foods high in fiber. The fibers knit themselves into a net and enmesh the calories, thereby preventing their absorption.

Fractions are non-fattening: half a hero sandwich, the bottom part of a layer cake, incomplete potato chips, broken cookies.

The word "just" automatically eliminates the calories in any food it's applied to, as in, "I'll **just** have a cheese Danish."

Leftovers have no calories regardless of what happens to them after they reach the kitchen. Anything placed in a doggy bag loses its calories regardless of whether the dog gets it . . . regardless of whether you own a dog.

Ingredients have no calories: banana slices intended for Jello and chocolate chips used in cookies do not acquire calories until the dish is complete.

Any food or ingredient that can fit on one finger is calorie free. Example: frosting. (Incidentally, cakes do not acquire calories until they are frosted.)

Anything "whole" is wholly without calories. Whole wheat bread is calorie free because the calories remain inside the grains and pass through your system intact.

Companionship foods are calorie free. (Note: these are foods eaten to keep someone else company. The person who asks you to join him in dessert is magnanimously offering to pick up your calorie tab.)

ALL FOREIGN FOODS ARE NON-FATTENING

Some examples on the following pages . . .

Pâté de fois gras (pa.tā de fwä'grä')
Fr. Literally, a paste of "false grass," a reference to its low calorie count. A rich-tasting pâté made principally of cottage cheese and de-fatted yogurt, cured to taste like goose liver. Approximate calories: 2 per tablespoon.

Pasta (päs'te) n. Italian de-calorized spaghetti, of which the principal type is made from semolina, containing only half the calories.

Baklava (bak'lë.vä' or bä. klä'vë) n. Turk.
Litterally, "baked lava," a Middle Eastern pastry in paper-thin layers with nuts, butter and honey, baked in specially designed stone ovens that cause the calories to go up in smoke. Approximate calories: 10 each.

Hollandaise (hol'en.dāz') v. To conceal in a sauce. Dutch method for reducing calorie count of food, adopted by French chefs. Based on the well known culinary principle that what you don't see can't hurt you. Also prevents shrinkage.

Fondue (fon.doo') n. Classic Swiss technique for lowering the calories in food by spearing it with decorative forks.

Shish kebab (shish'ke.bob') Turkish decalorization method, adapted from the Swiss.

Carafe (ke.raf) n. A glass decanter, used for lowering the calorie count in wine by translating it into liters.

Blintz (blints) Yid. A thin pancake that has been circumcised according to rabbinical law, to reduce calories. Calorie-free if filled with cottage cheese.

WHAT'S YOUR BODY TYPE?

Ectomorphs

Generally small boned, tall and slender. Rarely become obese.)
(See illustration)

Mesomorphs

Stocky and muscular, broad shoulders, powerful builds. Most of their weight is centered in the upper half of the torso.
(See illustration)

Endomorphs

Soft and rounded, gain weight easily. Differing from mesomorphs, their weight is usually centered in the lower half: with large hips and thighs, heavy legs, protruding abdomen.

There are also these subtypes:
Psychomorphs

Commonly known as "fatheads."

Jugomorphs

Are frontal mesomorphs, usually female. This type tends to develop large fat deposits over the pectoral muscles. In extreme cases, can interfere with typing.

Abdomorphs

Carry most of their weight in the laps. The first abdomorph cited in medical literature was Abner Gulch, the inventor of suspenders.

Pantomorphs

An extreme form of endomorph, characterized by heavy thighs and broad derrieres. On pantomorphs, all jeans are hip huggers.

Phobomorphs

A pantomorph with a neurotic fear of one-size-fits-all pantyhose.

Minkomorphs

Exact physiology is unknown; this type never removes her coat.

Tentomorphs

Southern climate variation, dresses in caftans and mu-mus.

Denimorphs

A concealed variant of an endomorph, size 14 and up, zipped into size 9 Calvin Klein jeans. Surgical removal may be necessary.

Polymorphs

People who are fat all over.

ARE YOU OVERWEIGHT?

The
answer
is yes
if . . .

- the post office has assigned you your own zip code
- you cause an eclipse when you hang your blue jeans on the clothes line
- you have to buy your suntan lotion in 50 gallon drums
- your new fur coat put mink on the endangered species list
- you qualify for group discounts
- the painters mistook your trenchcoat for a dropcloth
- you're the only person in the cafeteria who has a lunchbox on wheels
- Weight Watchers selected you as their poster boy
- the penny scale said you have no future
- the Smorgasbord restaurant got an injunction against you
- TWA added a surcharge to your plane ticket
- Lane Bryant took her catalog back

ARE YOU UNDERTALL?

Standard height-weight charts are incomplete. To find the proper height for your weight, consult the chart on the facing page.

DESIRABLE HEIGHTS

YOUR PRESENT WEIGHT	SMALL FRAME	MEDIUM FRAME	LARGE FRAME
185	6'3"	6'2"	6'1"
190	6'4"	6'3"	6'2"
200	6'5"	6'4"	6'3"
205	6'6"	6'5"	6'4"
210	6'7"	6'6"	6'5"
215	6'8"	6'7"	6'6"
220	6'9"	6'8"	6'7"
225	6'10"	6'9"	6'8"
230	6'11"	6'10"	6'9"
235	7'0"	6'11"	6'10"
240	7'1"	7'0"	6'11"
245	7'2"	7'1"	7'0"
250	7'3"	7'2"	7'1"
255	7'4"	7'3"	7'2"
260	7'5"	7'4"	7'3"
265	7'6"	7'5"	7'4"
270	7'7"	7'6"	7'5"
275	7'8"	7'7"	7'6"
280	7'9"	7'8"	7'7"
285	7'10"	7'9"	7'8"
290	7'11"	7'10"	7'9"
295	8'0"	7'11"	7'10"
300	8'1"	8'0"	7'11"

DO'S AND DON'TS FOR DRESSING SLIM

DO

wear wide belts

DON'T

wear horizontal stripes

DON'T

wear tight underwear that shows
bulge lines

DO
wear vertical stripes

DON'T
wear short shorts if you have flabby thighs

DON'T
wear turtlenecks if you have double chins

DO
wear the same color from head to toe, for a long unbroken line

DON'T
wear large plaids or patterns

DON'T
wear bulky fur coats or down jackets

DR. TURNOVERS

"Eat-all-you-can-get Diet"

You won't be hungry on this diet because you can have all you want. However, you must only eat the foods prescribed, no substitutes!

DAY ONE:

Breakfast
Jasmine tea (write for mail order address)
Litchee nuts
Fresh Peruvian pineapple
(Note: not Hawaiian)

Lunch
Radish Top and Turkey Gizzard Salad
Slovenian Salt Bread (see recipe)
Fresh figs

Snack
Goatsmilk-carob milkshake

Dinner
Kumquat Juice Cooler
Appetizer: caviar (Iranian)
Caribou Cutlet marinated in salt-free soy sauce
Fiddlehead Fern Salad with Rice Wine Vinegar Dressing
Baked, stuffed truffles
Homemade Crabapple Strudel

CUTTING CALORIES THE EASY WAY:

- Only eat the insides of sandwich cookies.
- Say a firm "No" to whipped cream on your hot fudge sundae, or carefully remove the maraschino cherry.
- Make your hot chocolate with skimmed milk.
- Scrape the icing numbers off your serving of birthday cake.
- Eat only the candies with fruit inside.
- Order vanilla.
- Buy a diet book.

THE EXCHANGE DIET

. . . is based on food trades.

For example, in place of
butter on your English muffin,
you may substitute two heaping
tablespoons of grape jam.

Memorize the
FOOD EQUIVALENTS
on the following pages:

If you skip the salad, you may substitute an equivalent amount of another cold food, Haagan Daaz caramel ice cream, for example.

If you fail to eat liver twice weekly, you may substitute two servings of another high iron food. (Note: chocolate covered raisins are a good choice.)

Zucchini left uneaten on your dinner plate must be replaced by an equivalent amount of another food of the same nationality. Lasagna or ravioli, for example.

If you pick out the peas and leave the carrots, the carrots may be replaced by another food of the same color, like orange sherbet. (Choose lime sherbet if you left the peas.)

All brown foods are interchangeable, lamb chops may be traded for chocolate layer cake, for example, or Hershey bars in place of whole wheat bread.

Food missed in the morning must be replaced later in the day. Cookies and chocolate milk before bedtime can stand in for today's skipped breakfast.

Unfinished food left behind in restaurants should be mentally assessed so that an equivalent amount of food can be added to the next meal eaten in private

It is not necessary to eat the baked potato if you consume the sour cream and bacon bits on top of it.

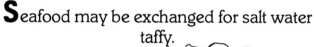

Seafood may be exchanged for salt water taffy.

If you don't like cottage cheese, you may substitute home fries.

AIDS
AND ADS
YOU
MAY HAVE
MISSED

(Low-classifieds)

COMPUTERIZED WEIGHTMATES

Why be lonely? Find love and happiness through computerized dating service for the obese. Include a 5 x 5 black and white photo.

Write to: Fat Friends, Inc.
Cellulite, Pa. 02437

SLIM DOWN THROUGH HYPNOSIS

Why struggle with starvation diets? This 10-week course will teach you how to hypnotize anybody, anywhere. Looking thin is in your power when you know how to put people in a trance!

Hip Hypnosis Associates
Thigh, N.C. 63702
1-800-444-6063

DIET WITH YOUR BOOTS ON

Ride the mechanical bully; pound your buns off! Come on down to Willy's Lonestar Diet Camp. A six-pack of lite beer with every meal.

ORDER THE SIZE YOU WANT TO BE

Gloria's specially constructed powernet de-signer jeans hug your waist, your hips, your thighs so tight you'll have a permanent smile on your face.
Phone now for immediate installation.)

Thigh, N.C. 63702
1-800-444-6063

LEARN HEAD OVER
HEELS YOGA from Shields Brooks.

Learn how to empty your mind and your closets,
develop the ability to converse with blue jeans.
Control your impulse to pluck your eyebrows.
Pay for this course with your rent money.

Write to: Shields Brookes
Box 734
Diaper, Michigan

DR. STILLWATER'S AMAZING
PERRIER DIET

Drink three glasses of imported water with every
meal. Develop muscle tone carrying home bottles.
Exhaust your food budget on water.

LOSE WEIGHT INSTANTLY

with this imported device . . . not available in American stores! Includes owner's manual in English,
explains why most Europeans weigh only half as
much as the typical American.
Send $10.95 to "Metric Scales."
        Kilo, Montana

HOW STEWARDESSES
STAY SLIM

Join the Airline Diner's Club. Enjoy gourmet entrees
like "Coq au Polyestre" and "Mousse aux Rouge
Deaux." Special introductory offer includes identifica-
tion chart to help you distinguish between the utensils
and the food. **Don't leave home without it.**

SLIMMERS' CRUISE ABOARD THE SS. MAL DE MER

Entertainment nightly: rock 'n' roll and swing 'n' sway your way to SLIMNESS. We guarantee you won't want to eat for a week!

BLOW YOURSELF UP

Enchanted photographer will create a lifesize poster from any favorite black and white photo (returned unharmed). Keep this poster in your attic and eat all you want. You remain slim while poster gains weight. **Write Dorian Gray Studios.**
Paintbrush, Oregon

FLATTEN YOUR STOMACH

Learn to play the accordian with Coach Jim Overreach. Free introductory lesson available on cassette or 8-track tape. Includes sheet music for Lady of Spain, Too Fat Polka, other perennial favorites. **Operators are waiting.**

Paintbrush, Oregon
1-800-22 Tootsie Goodbye

SLIM DOWN ON YOUR VACATION

Live in quaint native villages, lose weight while enjoying exotic foods. Special low charter airfares available. Book now with Third World Airlines.

THE CANADIAN RAT DIET

weight loss guaranteed! Rules out all food suspected of being carcinogenic. FDA approved!

ON SALE AT SUPERMARKET CHECK-OUTS

The Slimming Secrets of the Stars. Exclusive interviews with Liz, Shelley, Buddy, Orson and more!

FIND ROMANCE AT CLUB MESS

seven exotic locations, for overweights only. Two hundred pound minimum. Activities include muu-muu fashion shows, bake-offs, taffy-pulls, ice cream churning. Sample exotic native foods: whole roast boar, elephant drumsticks, camel hump fritters.

LOSE WEIGHT WITH EXTRA-TRIM CAPSULES

one is all you need! Simply clench the reusable capsule between your teeth during meal time . . . no prescription needed, no exercise, no dangerous drugs! From the same pharmaceutical company that brought you the knee grip birth control pill.

YOU LOSE WITH CELLU-LOSE!

In fact, your loss is guaranteed! Simply spend 10 minutes a day rubbing your unsightly bulges with this amazing sponge. Works equally well on thighs, buttocks, upper arms, midriff. **What have you got to lose? $9.95.**

LOSE 10-15 POUNDS IN ONE WEEK AT RANCHO MONTEZUMA

high in the hills overlooking Tijuana, Mexico. Partake in our famous cleansing water diet. Appetite loss guaranteed. First class accommodations, **private bathrooms.**

LOSE WEIGHT ADDRESSING ENVELOPES

Free details, Box 6.
Cellulite, PA. 02437

FAT CITY,

low rent housing project for the obese, funded by the FHA (Fat Housing Authority). You or your mate must be over 250 to qualify. Double-size dishwashers, 50 cubic foot freezers, Olympic-size bathtub, waddle-in closets. **Onsite shopping includes Fanny Farmer, Pizza Hut, Lane Bryant.**

WEIGHTWATCH-MEN, PART-TIME

Midnight shift, Hospital for the Criminally Obese. Guard candy machines.

ORIENTAL LIPOPUNCTURE REALLY WORKS!

Six surgically-trained Chinese tailors will stitch your lips shut. **Weight loss guaranteed.**

YOU, TOO, CAN BE SIZE FIVE

. . . or 7 or 9, all sizes available! Don't just tear out those incriminating size tags, replace them with the size you want to be. Please specify: ☐ sew-in ☐ iron-on ☐ check here to receive designer label catalog.

SPANDEX TAPE MEASURE

Str-r-r-etches to fit. Anyone can be a "10."
Or a 36-24-36.